SCHOLASTIC

Word Family Poetry Pages

KAMA EINHORN

New York · Toronto · London · Auckland · Sydney
Mexico City · New Delhi · Hong Kong · Buenos Aires

Teaching *Resources*

For a family who loves words:
Daniel and Jesse
and their parents, Rachel Schwarz and Marc Schiffman

Edited by Immacula A. Rhodes
Cover design by Maria Lilja
Interior design by Sydney Wright

ISBN: 978-0-545-24872-3

Contents

Poetry Pages

Short- and Long-a Phonograms

Short- and Long-e Phonograms

Short- and Long-i Phonograms

Short- and Long-o Phonograms

Short-u Phonograms

R-Controlled and Variant Vowel Phonograms

Reproducibles for Word Family Games & Activities

It's a Family Affair!

Word families, also known as phonograms, are a great way to recognize common spelling patterns. For instance, in the -at family, there's *bat, cat, hat, fat, sat, mat,* and so on. Almost 500 primary-grade words can be derived from a very small set of word families.

When children learn that words contain recognizable chunks that always sound the same, they've taken an important step on the road to reading fluency. Focusing on word families enhances children's understanding of how words work. As children begin to encounter longer words, they will quickly recognize these chunks. Quick recognition leads to faster decoding, which leads to increased fluency, which leads to better comprehension (when the brain is not focused on decoding, it is freed up for more higher-level thinking).

This book introduces, teaches, and reinforces 50 common word families. Each page focuses on a specific word family and invites children to write the phonogram on lines to make words that complete the poem. Children will benefit from the repeated practice in writing the phonograms on the lines and reading the resulting words.

These poems are great for flexible use and work well for any group configuration, whether whole group, small group, one-on-one, or independent. However you use each page, the final result is a fun, engaging poem with plenty of sight words and easy-to-decode words—perfect for read-aloud practice. Poems feature predictable, rhyming text and tie in to popular themes such as seasons, animals, shapes, all about me, feelings, and numbers. You'll even find some favorite familiar nursery rhymes and traditional poems and chants sprinkled throughout.

To further reinforce the target word family, an interactive extension activity based on the poem is provided at the bottom of each page. Children can use crayons or markers to complete these activities and personalize their learning.

With these fun, motivating poems, you'll enjoy watching children's reading confidence grow as they work their way though each page!

Using This Book

The word lists on pages 8–11 contain almost exclusively one-syllable words for the phonograms in this resource and are organized alphabetically by word family.

For each phonogram, the words are listed in alphabetical order: first by words that begin with a single consonant, then by words beginning with consonant blends or digraphs. It is helpful to introduce the single-consonant words before moving on to words with consonant blends or digraphs.

Each poetry page in this book represents one of the 50 word families on the list. Simply reproduce the pages and give them to children to create their very own word family poem and picture. You might follow these five steps:

1 Give each child a copy of the same page. Ask: *What word family do you see on this page?* (Children can find the target word family at the top right corner of the page.)

2 Now say: *This poem is missing some important words. Write the word family on the lines to finish the words. Then you'll have a complete poem.*

3 Read the completed poem aloud as a group. Encourage children to track the print with their fingers. Read the poem aloud several times until all children are reading along fluently.

4 Introduce the activity at the bottom of the page and encourage children to complete it with crayons or colored pencils.

5 Children might keep all their completed word family poem pages in a folder. When they have completed all 50 poems, the pages can be bound together into a book for children to take home and read with their families.

Word Family Games & Activities

**Use the word banks on pages 8–11 for any
of these games and activities.**

Word Family Forest

Choose about four word families and write several words from each on index cards (one word per card). Then distribute the cards—one per child. Have children stand in an open space. When you say "Word Family Forest!" children find the other members of their "family tree" and stand together. When all "family trees" have gathered, stand near each one and have each child read his or her word aloud.

Poem Scramble

Take one completed poem page and cut the lines of the poem apart into strips. Challenge children to put the strips back into the order of the original poem. Try the same thing using individual lines of the poem only (cut apart the words and have children put them in order to recreate the line).

Make a Word

Use magnetic letters or a flannel board and felt pieces to create the words in any word family of your choice. Let children manipulate the letters to form all the words in that list.

Word Family Listening Center

Tape-record selected word family poems and let children listen to them in the listening center as they read along.

Word Family Poets

Challenge children to make up their own original poems, independently or collaboratively, using the words in one word family list. Have a poetry reading!

Pocket-Chart Families

Write each line (minus the target word) from the poem on a sentence strip. Using a different color marker, write the missing target words on index cards, labeling each card with a different word. Have children help you reconstruct the poem and put the strips and cards in the right places in a pocket chart. Read the completed poem together, tracking the print with your finger or a pointer. You might also invite a child to track the print for the group.

Duck, Muck, Luck!

Play this adapted game just as you would "Duck, Duck, Goose," but use word family words. Tell children which trigger word to listen for. For instance:

Duck, muck, stuck . . . *luck*!

Bump, lump, pump . . . *jump*!

Ring, sing, thing . . . *zing*!

Cap, tap, flap . . . *zap*!

Dock, rock, sock . . . *shock*!

Mystery Word

After children are very familiar with a poem, have them turn their papers over so they cannot see it. Read the poem aloud, pausing when you come to a word family word. Challenge children to call out the word that belongs there. If they need help, you can give them the first letter in the word.

Three Cheers for Word Families

Copy pages 62 and 63 for each child. (Page 62 is for two-letter phonograms like -*ap*, and page 63 is for three-letter phonograms like -*ake*.) Help children choose an appropriate word family to use in the cheer. Then have them fill in the word family and words to complete the cheer. Finally, invite children to share their cheer and lead the class in reciting it a few times together.

Word Family Tree

Distribute a copy of page 64 to children. Invite them to write a word family at the top of the tree. Then have them fill in the blanks with words belonging to that word family.

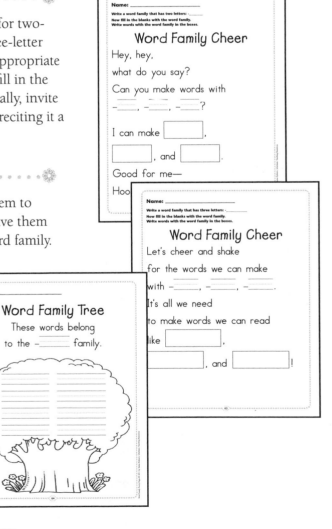

Word Banks

-ab
cab
dab
fab
gab
jab
lab
nab
tab
blab
crab
drab
flab
grab
scab
stab

-ack
back
hack
lack
pack
rack
sack
tack
black
clack
crack
quack
shack
slack
smack
snack
stack
track
whack
knack

-ad
bad
dad
fad
had
lad
mad
pad
sad
tad
clad

glad
grad

-ail
bail
fail
hail
jail
mail
nail
pail
rail
sail
tail
wail
flail
frail
quail
snail
trail

-ain
main
pain
rain
vain
brain
chain
drain
grain
plain
slain
sprain
stain
strain
train

-ake
bake
cake
fake
lake
make
rake
sake
take
wake
brake
drake

flake
quake
shake
snake
stake

-ale
bale
gale
male
pale
sale
tale
scale
stale
whale

-all
all
ball
call
fall
hall
mall
tall
wall
small
squall
stall

-ame
came
dame
fame
game
lame
name
same
tame
blame
flame
frame
shame

-an
an
ban
can
fan

man
pan
ran
tan
van
bran
clan
plan
scan
span
than

-ank
bank
lank
rank
sank
tank
yank
blank
clank
crank
drank
flank
plank
prank
spank
thank

-ap
cap
gap
lap
map
nap
rap
sap
tap
yap
zap
chap
clap
flap
scrap
slap
snap
strap
trap
wrap

-are
bare
care
dare
fare
hare
mare
pare
rare
ware
blare
flare
glare
scare
share
snare
spare
square
stare

-ash
bash
cash
dash
gash
hash
lash
mash
rash
sash
brash
clash
flash
slash
smash
stash
thrash
trash

-at
bat
cat
fat
hat
mat
pat
rat
sat
vat
brat
chat
flat
gnat
spat

splat
that

-ate
date
fate
gate
hate
late
mate
rate
crate
grate
plate
skate
state

-aw
caw
jaw
law
paw
raw
saw
claw
draw
flaw
slaw
squaw
straw
gnaw

-ay
bay
day
gay
hay
jay
lay
may
nay
pay
ray
say
way
clay
fray
gray
play
pray
slay
spray
stay
stray
tray

-eat
beat
feat
heat
meat
neat
peat
seat
bleat
cheat
cleat
pleat
treat
wheat

-ed
bed
fed
led
red
wed
bled
bred
fled
shed
shred
sled
sped

-eed
deed
feed
heed
need
reed
seed
weed
bleed
creed
freed
greed
speed
tweed

-eep
beep
deep
jeep
keep
peep
seep
weep
cheep
creep

sheep
sleep
steep
sweep

-ell
bell
cell
dell
fell
jell
nell
sell
tell
well
yell
swell
shell
smell
spell
swell

-end
end
bend
fend
lend
mend
send
tend
vend
blend
spend
trend

-est
best
jest
lest
nest
pest
rest
test
vest
west
zest
chest
crest
quest
guest
wrest

-ice
ice
dice
lice
mice
nice
rice
vice
price
slice
spice
thrice
twice

-ick
kick
lick
pick
sick
tick
wick
brick
chick
click
flick
quick
slick
stick
thick
trick

-ide
hide
ride
side
tide
wide
bride
glide
pride
slide
snide
stride

-ight
fight
light
might
night
right
sight
tight
blight
bright

flight
fright
plight
knight

-ill
ill
bill
dill
fill
gill
hill
kill
mill
pill
sill
till
will
chill
drill
frill
grill
quill
skill
spill
still
thrill
trill
twill

-in
in
bin
fin
kin
pin
tin
win
chin
grin
shin
skin
spin
thin
twin

-ine
dine
fine
line
mine
nine
pine
vine

shine
shrine
spine
swine
whine

-ing
bing
ding
king
ping
ring
sing
wing
zing
bring
cling
fling
sling
spring
sting
string
swing
thing
wring

-ink
ink
kink
link
mink
pink
rink
sink
wink
blink
brink
clink
drink
shrink
slink
stink
think

-ip
dip
hip
lip
nip
rip
sip
tip
zip
blip

chip
clip
drip
flip
grip
quip
ship
skip
slip
snip
strip
trip
whip

-it
it
bit
fit
hit
kit
lit
pit
sit
wit
flit
grit
quit
skit
slit
spit
split
knit

-oat
oat
boat
coat
goat
moat
bloat
float
gloat
throat

-ock
dock
hock
lock
mock
rock
sock
tock
block
clock

crock
flock
frock
shock
smock
stock
knock

-oke
coke
joke
poke
woke
yoke
broke
choke
smoke
spoke
stoke
stroke

-op
bop
cop
hop
mop
pop
sop
top
chop
crop
drop
flop
plop
prop
shop
slop

-ore
bore
core
fore
gore
more
pore
sore
tore
wore
chore
score
shore
snore
spore

store
swore

-ose
hose
nose
pose
rose
chose
close
prose
those

-ot
cot
dot
got
hot
jot
lot
not
pot
rot
tot
blot
clot
plot
shot
slot
spot
trot
knot

-ow
bow
low
mow
row
sow
tow
blow
crow
flow
glow
grow
show
slow
snow
stow
know

-ub
cub
dub

hub
nub
rub
sub
tub
club
flub
grub
scrub
shrub
snub
stub

-uck
buck
duck
luck
muck
puck
suck
tuck
cluck
pluck
stuck
struck
truck

-ug
bug
dug
hug
jug
lug
mug
pug
rug
tug
chug
drug
plug
shrug
slug
smug
snug
thug

-ump
bump
dump
hump
jump
lump
pump
rump

chump
clump
frump
grump
plump
slump
stump
thump
trump

-unk
bunk
dunk
hunk
junk
sunk
chunk
drunk
flunk
plunk
shrunk
skunk
slunk
spunk
stunk
trunk

-ush
gush
hush
lush
mush
rush
blush
brush
crush
flush
plush
slush
thrush

Name: _____

Write the word family on the lines.

Gabby the Crab

Gabby the Crab___

just loves to g___.

He thinks he's so f___.

He loves to bl___.

"Bl___, bl___, bl___!"

g___s Gabby the cr___.

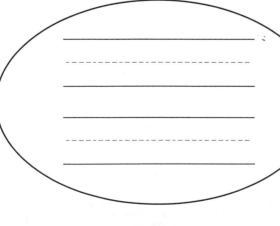

Color Gabby the **Crab**. What two **-ab** words would you like for him to say? Write them in the speech bubble.

Name: _____

Write the word family on the lines.

Mack's Snack Shack

M̲a̲c̲k̲ really has a kn̲_____

for making pancakes in a st̲_____.

He will put them in a s̲_____

and let you carry them b̲_____,

so you can have them at home

for a yummy late-night sn̲_____.

Mack's Snack Shack

Help **Mack** paint the sign for his **snack shack**.
Use the color **black** somewhere in the sign.

Write the word family on the lines.

Feelings

Brad felt m____.

T____ felt s____.

They both felt b____,

but Ch____ felt gl____.

M____, s____, b____, gl____ —

these are all feelings

that the friends h____.

Draw a picture
of something
that might make
Chad feel **glad**.

Name: _____

Write the word family on the lines.

A Plan and a Van

D̲a̲n̲ is a m____

with a pl____.

St____ is a m____

with a v____.

What might these two do,

D____ with his pl____

and St____ with his v____?

Draw what you think **Dan** and **Stan**
might do with their **plan** and their **van**.

Name: _____

Write the word family on the lines.

Thank You!

Put a penny in the b ank .

Feed the fish in the t_____.

Fix the floor

with the broken pl_____ —

just give it

a nice big y_____.

For all the things

that you do,

I th_____ you!

Draw a picture to show the last
time you said "**thank** you."

16

Write the word family on the lines.

Zap the Firefly

Z̲a̲p̲ didn't want to n_____.

He wanted to fl_____

and sn_____ and y_____.

But soon Z_____

was a tired little ch_____,

so he turned off his light

and took a n_____,

snuggled deep

in his p_____'s l_____.

Color **Zap** the Firefly.

Name: _____

Write the word family on the lines.

Birthday Bash

Bam! Crash!

Boom! Cl____!

Bang! Sm____!

Why all the noise, you ask?

I'm getting pans to make a cake

for your giant birthday b____!

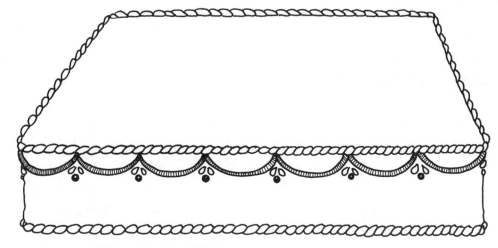

Decorate the cake for your own birthday **bash**.

Name: _____

Write the word family on the lines.

Pat the Bat

Meet Pat the B___,

and her friends, C___ and R___.

But whatever you do,

don't step on her m___ . . .

P___ the B___

doesn't like th___.

Pat's Mat

Color **Pat's mat** any way you like.

Name: _____

Write the word family on the lines.

Two Snails

One sn**ail** goes to get the m_____.

Another sn_____ picks

flowers to put in a p_____.

Each sn_____ stops

to watch a boat lift its s_____.

Then each sn_____ moves

along its own little tr_____.

Color each **snail** purple.
Color each **trail** green.

Name: _____

Write the word family on the lines.

I Love Trains

I love riding on a tr__ain__,

hearing "choo choo"

in my br_____.

In the sun or pouring r_____,

fast or slow, fancy or pl_____—

I love riding on a tr_____!

Color the **train**. Then add some **rain**!

21

Name: _____

Write the word family on the lines.

ake

Make a Cake

Find sugar and flour,

whatever it t_ake_s.

Mix them together,

for goodness s_____!

Put the batter in the oven

and let it b_____.

That's how you m_____

a yummy c_____!

Draw a **cake** you would like to **make**.

22

Name: _____

Write the word family on the lines.

Whale on a Scale

Don't let a wh__ale__

stand on your sc_____.

If it does, you'll turn p_____,

and end up with a t_____

of how a wh_____

broke your sc_____!

How many pounds do you think the **whale** weighs?
Write the number next to the **scale**. Then color the picture.

Name: _____

Write the word family on the lines.

Game Room

Come play a g_ame_.

Do you know everyone's n_____?

Play the n_____ g_____.

Can you make a lion behave?

Play the t_____ g_____.

Do you want to play again?

play the s_____ g_____!

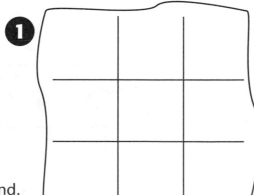

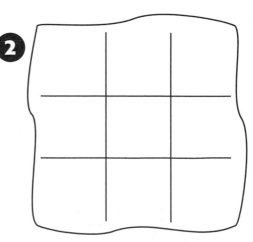

Play tic-tac-toe with a friend.
Who won each **game**?

Name: _____

Write the word family on the lines.

Kate and Nate

K__ate__ and N_____

love to sk_____,

and they h_____ to stop.

But show them spaghetti and

gr_____ cheese on top—

they'll take a pl_____

and sit down with a flop.

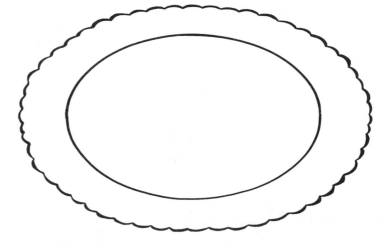

Draw spaghetti on the **plate**.
What else might you eat with spaghetti?
Draw that too.

Name: _____

Write the word family on the lines.

Go Away, Rain!

Rain, rain, go aw___ay___.

The children s_____

they want to pl_____.

Sun, Sun, come and st_____.

The children s_____

They're tired of gr_____!

Draw what you might do on
a rainy **day** and on a sunny **day**.

Name: _____

Write the word family on the lines.

Red, Red, Red

N͟e͟d͟ had a r_____ b_____.

T_____ had a r_____ sl_____.

Fr_____ had a r_____ sh_____.

N_____, T_____, Fr_____.

B_____, sl_____, sh_____.

R_____, r_____, r_____!

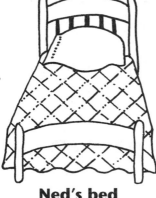

Ned's bed

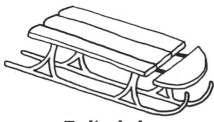

Ted's sled

Fred's shed

Color Ned's bed, Ted's sled, and Fred's shed.
Use red. Then draw something of yours that is red.

Name: _____

Write the word family on the lines.

Spelling Test

Tell me, t____ me:

Can you sp____ b____?

Can you sp____ f____?

Can you sp____ s____?

Can you sp____ sh____?

Give a great big y____!

You can sp____

very w____!

What else can you do **well**?
Draw it here.

Name: _____

Write the word family on the lines.

Spelling Tricks

Read this word: b<u>end</u>.

Add an *l*: bl_____.

Read this word: s_____.

Add a *p*: sp_____.

B_____, bl_____.

S_____, sp_____.

Now you're at the very _____!

To whom do you want
to **send** a letter in the mail?
Write the person's name and
decorate the envelope.

Name: _____

Write the word family on the lines.

The Nest of -est

The n<u>est</u> of – ____

is really the b_____.

Each bird wears

a cool feather v_____.

If you've flown in

far from the w_____,

then come in, sit,

and have a r_____!

Draw yourself having a **rest** in the **nest**.

30

Name: _____

Write the word family on the lines.

Beat the Heat

How can you b eat

summer h_____, h_____, h_____?

Have an ice pop

for a tr_____, tr_____, tr_____.

Then jump in the pool—

N_____, n_____, n_____!

Draw something you do to **beat** the **heat**.

Name: _____

Write the word family on the lines.

Plant a Seed

Plant a s__eed__.

Pull a w_____.

What else does a garden n_____?

Soil, sun, water, and time.

A gardener works hard—

there are people to f_____.

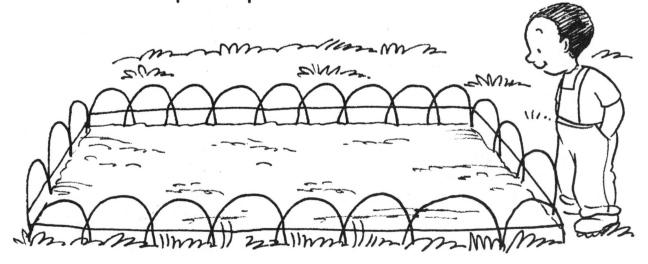

Draw vegetables in the garden.
Draw some **weeds**, too!

Counting Sheep

If you really can't sleep,

then try to count sh_____ .

Keep counting sh_____

'til you fall asl_____ .

But don't count baby birds—

they'll keep you awake,

because they p_____

and ch_____ and ch_____ !

Color the **sheep**. Then count them.

Name: _____

Write the word family on the lines.

Sick Rick

My dog R ick got s_____.

He wouldn't chase his st_____

or do his tr_____.

Then Dr. N_____ pulled

a t_____ off of R_____!

And R_____ felt better

very qu_____.

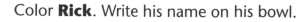

Color Rick. Write his name on his bowl.

34

Name: _____

Write the word family on the lines.

The Hill of -ill

What will you do

on the H____ of -ill?

You w____ see Jack,

and you w____ see J____.

You w____ even help

cook on the gr____.

The H____ of -ill

is really a thr____!

Hill
of -ill

What else **will** you do on the **Hill** of -**ill**? Draw it here.

Name: _____

Write the word family on the lines.

Chicken Pox!

I have so many

all over my sk<u>in</u>.

I've got six of them

just on my ch_____.

I'm itching so badly,

it makes my head sp_____!

Draw something that might make your head **spin!**

Name: _____

Write the word family on the lines.

Sing, Bird!

Sing, bird, s_____.

It's time for spr_____.

The flap of your w_____,

and the song that you s_____

will br_____ z_____

to everyth_____.

Then I can play

all day on my sw_____.

Help the bird **sing** for **spring**. Color in the notes.

Name: _____

Write the word family on the lines.

Wink and Blink

One eye can wink.

Two eyes can bl____.

Can you, can you

w____ and bl____?

Tell me what you

th____, th____, th____.

Color in the eyes to match your eye color.
Cover up one eye and say "**wink**."
Cover both eyes and say "**blink**."

Name: _____

Write the word family on the lines.

A Trip to Blip

Take a trip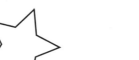

to Planet Bl____.

Zoom around

in a spacesh____.

You'll love it there.

You'll really fl____!

What does Planet **Blip** look like?
Color the circle to look like **Blip**.

Name: _____

Write the word family on the lines.

In the City of -it

In the trees, you can see

the butterflies fl___.

At the diner, you can make

a banana spl___.

On the park benches,

you can s___ and kn___,

You can do all of this

in the City of -it!

What would you like to do in the City of **-it**?
Draw **it** in the box.

Name: _____

Write the word family on the lines.

Soup Is Nice

On cold nights, soup is n ice .

First boil water.

Get vegetables to d_____.

Add some r_____,

then find some sp_____.

Stir once, stir tw_____.

Mmmm, that's n_____!

What might be **nice** to put in your soup?
Draw the items around the pot.

41

Name: _____

Write the word family on the lines.

Slide, Glide, Hide

Penguins on ice sl____.

Birds in the air gl____.

Turtles in their shells h____.

Kids on their bikes r____.

This all happens

outs____, outs____.

Draw something that you do **outside**.

Name: _____

Write the word family on the lines.

Wishing

Star light, star br_____.

First star I see

at n_____.

I wish I may,

I wish I m_____

have the wish

I wish this n_____.

Color the star a **bright** color.
Then draw what you wish for.

Name: _____

Write the word family on the lines.

Number Nine

Here comes special Number N ine .

Going down the railroad l_____.

When she's polished,

she will sh_____.

There goes special

Number N_____!

Trace the number **nine** on the train.
Then color the train.

Name: _____

Write the word family on the lines.

Tick Tock

My play date is at 2 o'clock.

At the door I hear a kn_____!

We build a tower

bl_____ by bl_____.

And make a puppet

from a s_____.

I don't want

the fun to stop.

Tick, t_____,

tick, t_____.

Draw something you might be doing at two **o'clock**.

Name: _____

Write the word family on the lines.

The Land of -op

There's a place where you

can watch popcorn p op ,

or h____ on a hill

way up to the t____.

Even when you're ready to dr____,

in the Land of -op,

you just can't st____!

Color the sign.
Then draw a **shop** at the **top** of the hill.

Name: _____

Write the word family on the lines.

Dot's Spots

Dot the Leopard

is proud of each sp____.

They're small and black,

like a domino d____!

Sp____, d____, sp____, d____.

D____ the Leopard

really has quite a l____.

**Draw dots and spots
on Dot the Leopard.**

47

Name: _____

Write the word family on the lines.

Row Your Boat

Row, row, row your b<u>oat</u>

gently in the lake.

Don't forget

to wear your c_____.

It's cold,

for goodness' sake!

Draw yourself in the **boat**.
Don't forget your **coat**!

A Joke?

I woke up when I felt a p oke .

My sister sp_____:

"It's just a j_____!"

I told her "No . . .

a p_____ is really NOT a j_____!"

My Joke

Draw or write a **joke** or something funny in this book.

Name: _____

Write the word family on the lines.

Choosing a Rose

I was supposed

to pick a r<u>ose</u>.

I didn't know

which r_____ to pick.

But my n_____,

it ch_____ a r_____,

and that's the r_____

I ch_____ to pick!

Color the **rose** your **nose** might pick.

Write the word family on the lines.

Growing Words

Do you kn__ow__ about -ow?

There's a garden of words,

it can help you gr_____:

B_____, l_____, t_____, sl_____.

Bl_____, cr_____, gl_____, fl_____.

Inch by inch, r_____ by r_____,

-ow can make a garden gr_____.

know, bow, tow, tow,

slow, blow, crow, grow

Make the garden **grow**. Trace the **-ow** words.

51

Name: _____

Write the word family on the lines.

The Clean Cub Club

R___-a-d___-d___,

Three c___s in a t___.

Scr___, scr___, scr___—

They're the clean c___ cl___!

Color the **cubs** in the **tub**.

Name: _____

Write the word family on the lines.

Chuck and Huck

Ch_____'s tr_____

got st_____ in m_____.

Chuck said, "I'm out of l_____."

Then along came H_____

with a tow tr_____.

Chuck's
Trucking

And he pulled

the st_____ tr_____

out of the m_____.

Huck's
Towing

Color **Chuck's truck** red.
Color **Huck's** tow **truck** yellow.

Name: _____

Write the word family on the lines.

A Snug Bug

How does a b__ug__

get sn_____ in a r_____?

First he drinks cocoa

from a nice warm m_____.

Then from his dad,

he gets a big h_____.

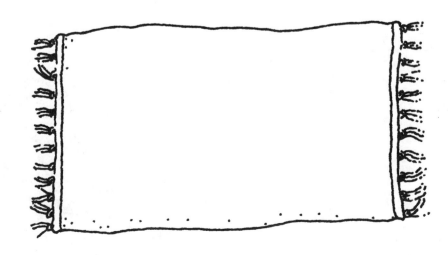

Draw a **bug** in the **rug**.

Bumpy the Hippo

Bumpy the hippo

is big and pl___ump___.

Bumpy runs

and takes a j_____ . . .

Bumpy makes

a great big th_____!

J_____, b_____!

Th_____, b_____!

Color **Bumpy** the Hippo. Then **thump**
your hand on your desk when you
are finished. **Thump, thump, thump!**

Name: _____

Write the word family on the lines.

Chocolate Dunks

I can make good cookies.

I call them "chocolate d__unk__s."

I take a h_____ of chocolate,

and cut it into ch_____s.

I bake the cookies, get some milk . . .

and d_____, d_____, d_____!

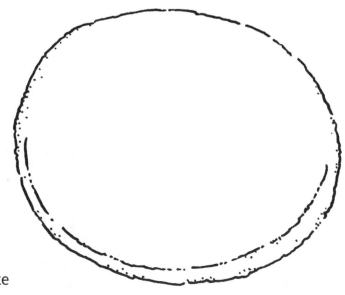

Draw **chunks** of chocolate
in this cookie.

Winter Hush

On a cold winter night,

through snow and slush,

r_____ home, r_____ home,

in the dark's chilly h_____.

Draw yourself as you **rush** home.

Name: _____

Write the word family on the lines.

Play Ball!

Throw your b̲a̲l̲l̲
_____
against the w_____ .

_____

Bounce your b_____

_____

down the h_____ .

_____

Listen up, hear the c_____ :

_____   _____

"Play b_____ , play b_____ !"

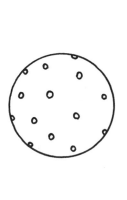

Color each **ball**. Then draw your own **ball**.

Name: _____

Write the word family on the lines.

Square City

In Squ<u>are</u> City, people sh_____.

They are kind, they really c_____.

And everything is really squ_____!

Do you have a squ_____

to sp_____?

Sh_____ your squ_____—

show you c_____!

Draw a house you might see in **Square** City.
Use only **squares** to make the house.

The -aw Café

At the greatest place

you ever saw,

you can eat

the best cole sl_____.

Paper's on the table

where you can dr_____.

And each drink comes

with a curly str_____ —

here, it's the l_____!

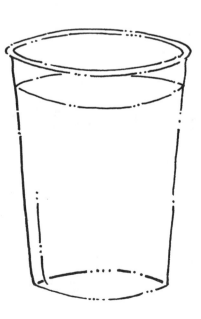

Draw a curly **straw** in the glass.

Name: _____

Write the word family on the lines.

Snore or Adore?

It makes me sn_ore_

when all is a b_____,

when I'm sick at home

and my throat is s_____.

But here's what I ad_____:

Going out to expl_____,

shopping in a st_____,

and fun games

when I keep sc_____.

Draw something you **adore**.

Write a word family that has two letters: -_____ ____

Now fill in the blanks with the word family.
Write words with the word family in the boxes.

Word Family Cheer

Hey, hey,

what do you say?

Can you make words with

-_____, -_____, -_____?

I can make [   ],

[   ], and [   ].

Good for me—

Hooray! Hooray!

Name: _____

Write a word family that has three letters: -_____ _____ _____

Now fill in the blanks with the word family.

Write words with the word family in the boxes.

Word Family Cheer

Let's cheer and shake

for the words we can make

with -_____, -_____, -_____.

It's all we need

to make words we can read

like [   ],

[   ], and [   ]!

Word Family Tree

These words belong
to the – _____ family.